OLIVER LEARNS

ABOUT RACISM

OLIVER LEARNS

ABOUT RACISM

A LEWKOR SACKS BOOK

If you email me, I'll send you more information on talking to your child about racism.*

At the end of this book.

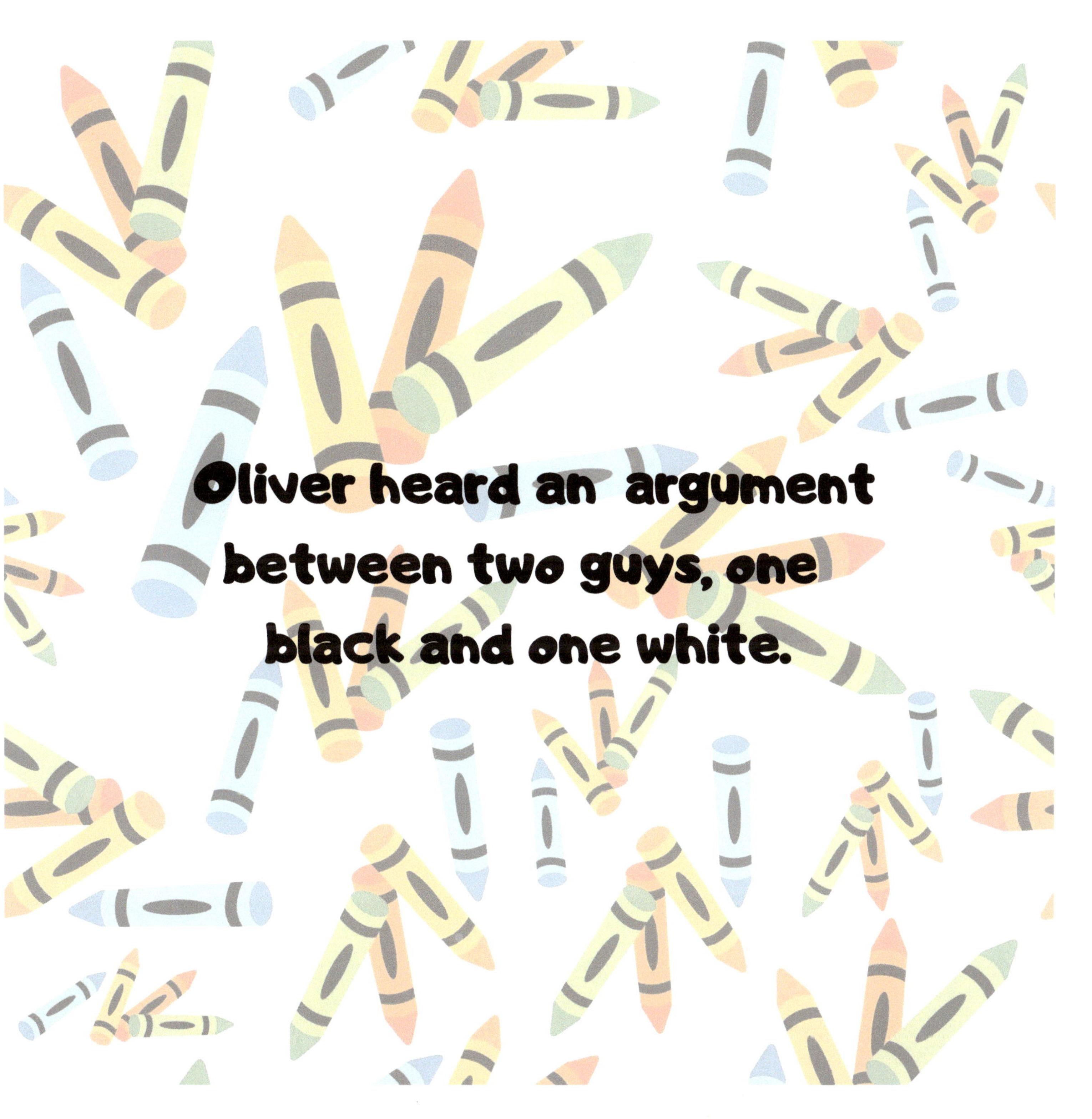
Oliver heard an argument between two guys, one black and one white.

His parents explained the problem called racism. Oliver had five dreams that night.

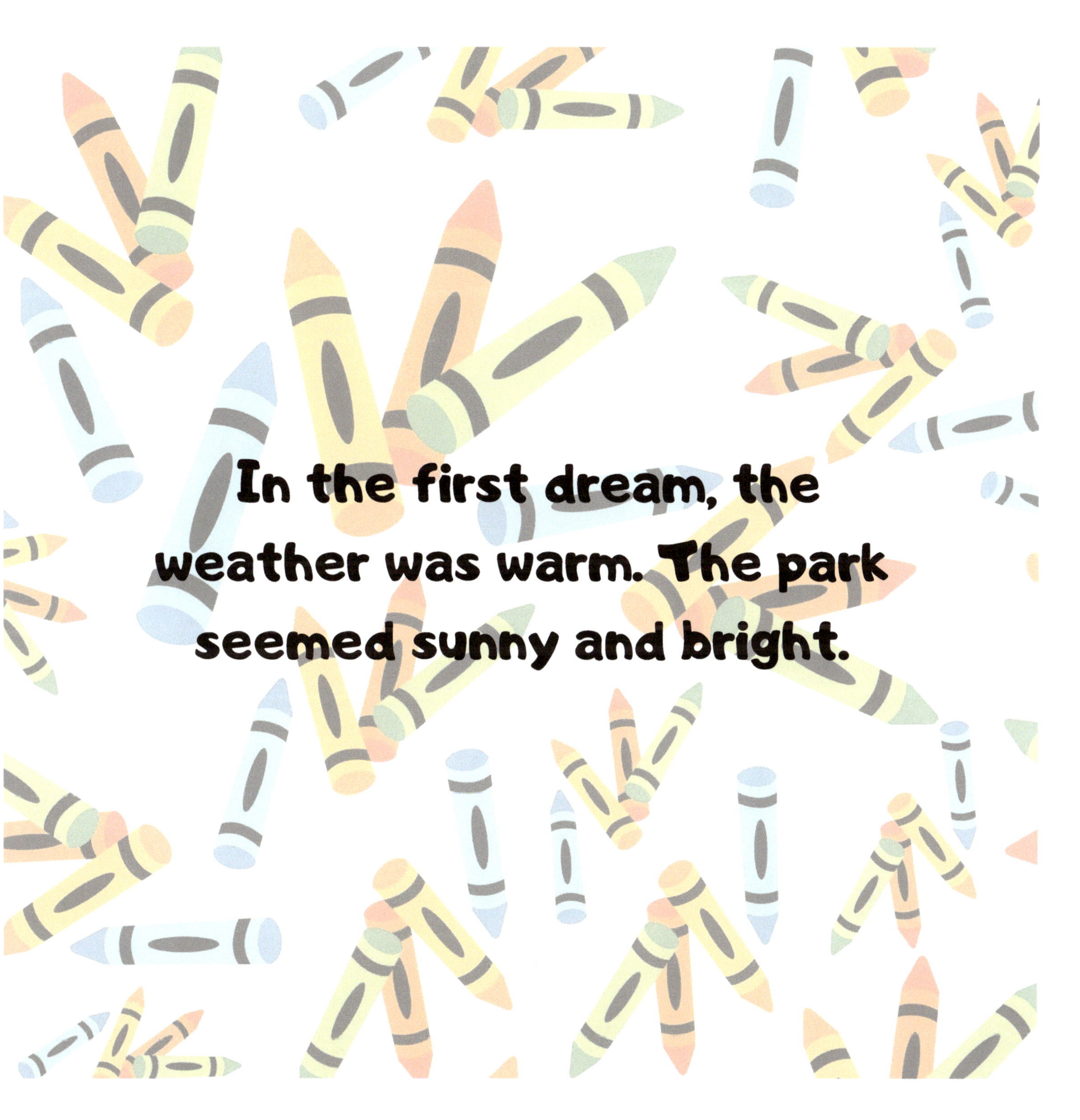
In the first dream, the weather was warm. The park seemed sunny and bright.

Oliver decided to
draw his friends as
they ran and played.

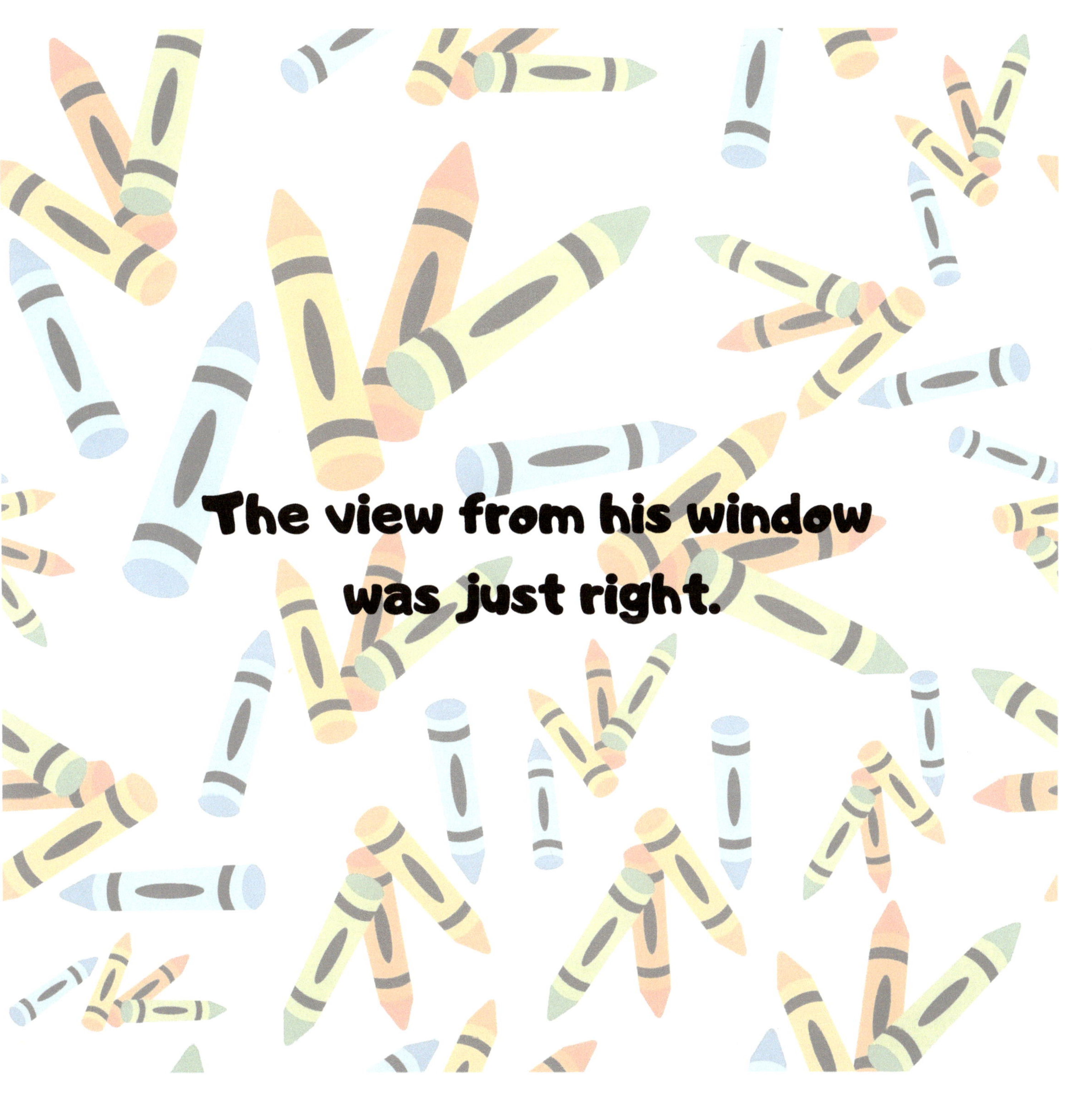
The view from his window
was just right.

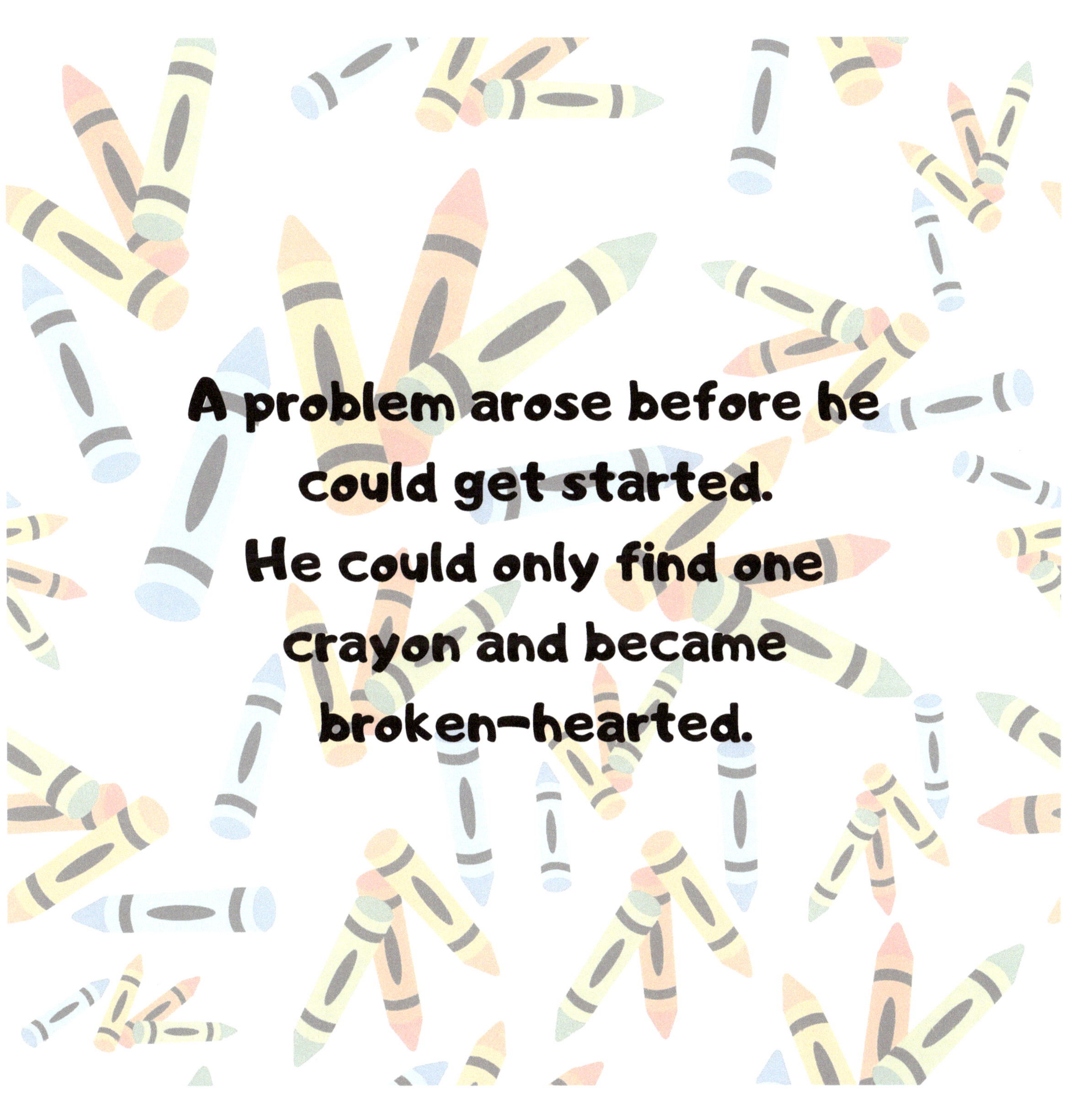
A problem arose before he could get started.
He could only find one crayon and became broken-hearted.

With a white
crayon, he drew
all he could see.

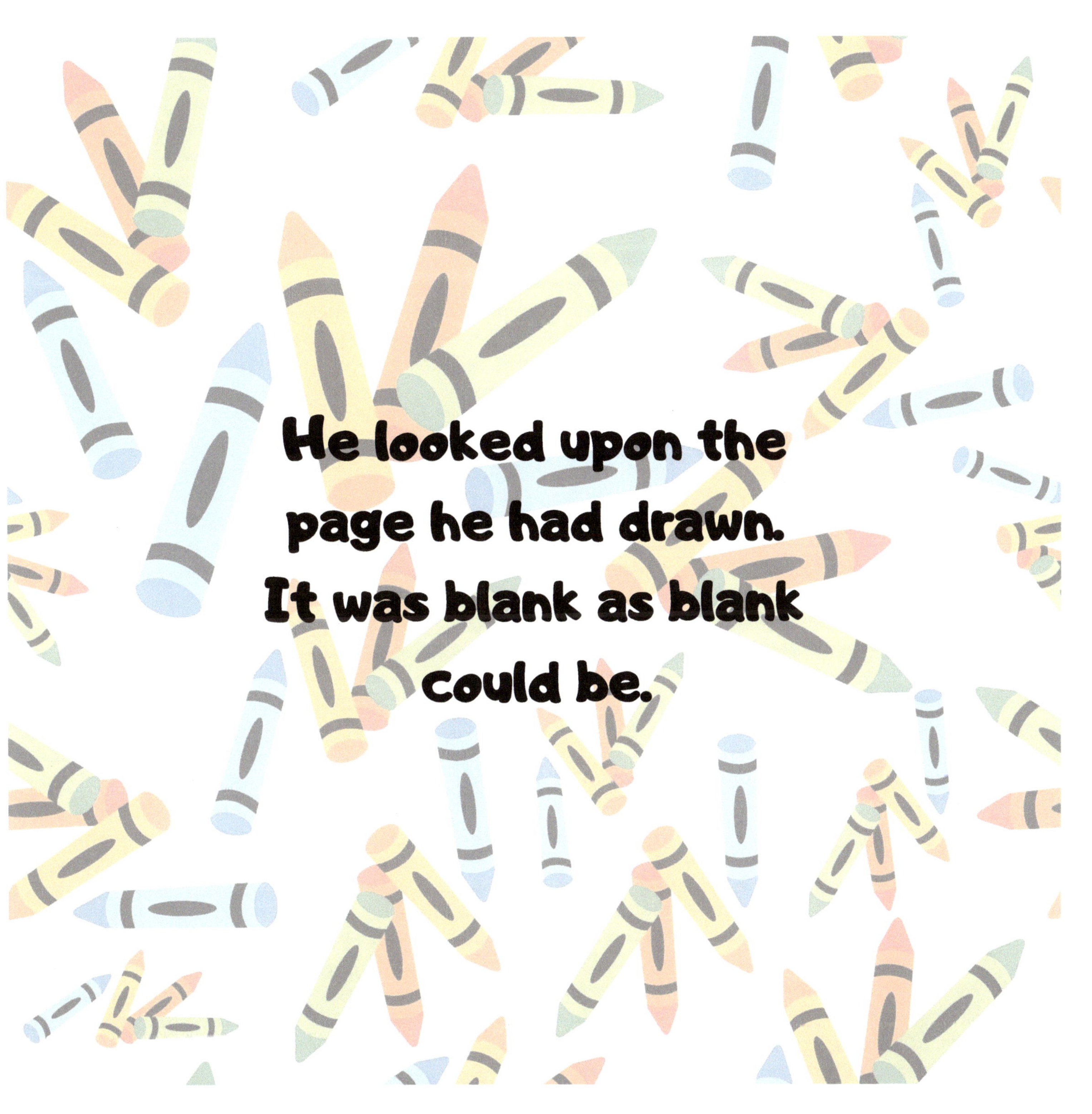

He looked upon the
page he had drawn.
It was blank as blank
could be.

In the second
dream, Oliver
found a green
crayon and drew
the park again,

But the sky was green, the trees were green, and so were all his friends.

Oliver wasn't happy
and searched his room
again,

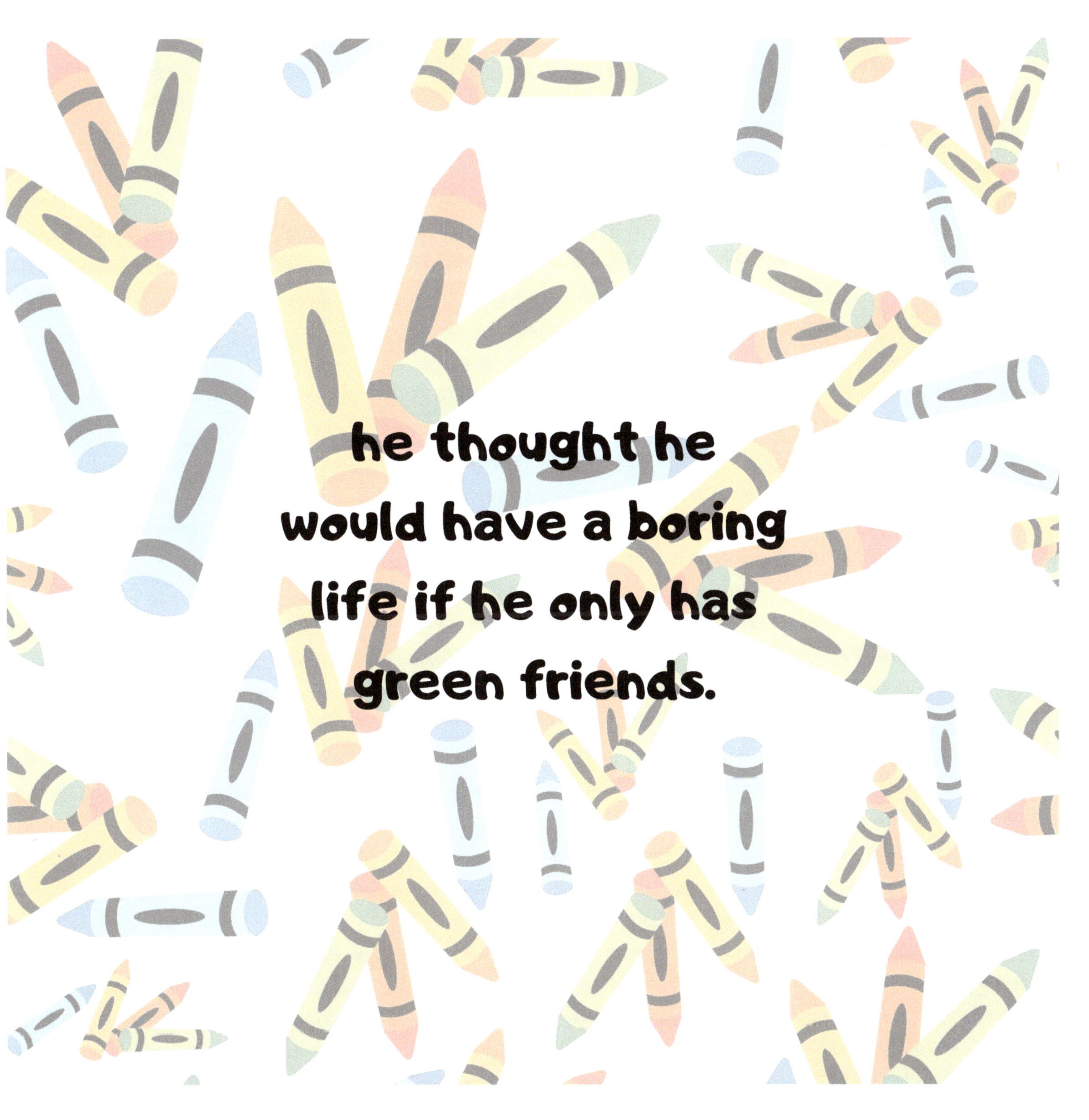
he thought he
would have a boring
life if he only has
green friends.

In the third
dream, he found a
red crayon and
drew his friends
having fun.

It still did not look very nice with red friends, a red sky and a red sun.

In the fourth
dream he
used a blue
crayon,

the sky
seemed just
right,

But not the blue clouds, blue sun, blue trees and a friend who was flying a blue kite.

In the fifth dream, Oliver
looked upon his page and
knew just what to do.

He searched for all his crayons and a blank page or two.

Oliver drew a blue
sky, puffy white
clouds and beautiful
birds in the air.

He drew a picture of his best friend, Bill. He has brown skin and curly black hair.

Racism means some
people believe one
color is better than
the rest.

But Oliver learned it takes all colors to see our world at its best.

THE END

OR Actually,
The Beginning
of the World
Healing

THANK YOU
FOR TAKING
A FIRST
STEP TO END
RACISM

If you email me,
I'll send you more
information on
talking to your
child about
racism.
LEWIS@DRCLRILEYSR.COM

PLEASE
LEAVE A
COMMENT
ON AMAZON
AND GOOD
READS.
THANK YOU

MORE
LEWKOR
SACKS
BOOKS TO
COME

RACISM IS BAD